ideals
AUTUMN

Autumn is the gold embrace,
The amber aftermath
Of summer's swift, impetuous race
Across a primrose path.

Autumn is the fragrant fire
Of the hillside's vibrant glow
That the leafen-love of spring desire
Set greening a season ago.

Autumn is the mellow mood
Once rash and summer-willed,
The shy, young dream that April wooed,
Now autumn-wise fulfilled.

Marilyn Eynon Scott

ISBN 0-8249-1013-3 350

IDEALS—Vol. 39, No. 6 September MCMLXXXII IDEALS (ISSN 0019-137X) is published eight times a year,
February, March, April, June, August, September, November, December
by IDEALS PUBLISHING CORPORATION, 11315 Watertown Plank Road, Milwaukee, Wis. 53226
Second class postage paid at Milwaukee, Wisconsin. Copyright © MCMLXXXII by IDEALS PUBLISHING CORPORATION.
POSTMASTER: Send address changes to Ideals, Post Office Box 2100, Milwaukee, Wis. 53201
All rights reserved. Title IDEALS registered U.S. Patent Office.
Published simultaneously in Canada.

ONE YEAR SUBSCRIPTION—eight consecutive issues as published—$15.95
TWO YEAR SUBSCRIPTION—sixteen consecutive issues as published—$27.95
SINGLE ISSUE—$3.50

The cover and entire contents of IDEALS are fully protected by copyright and must
not be reproduced in any manner whatsoever. Printed and bound in U.S.A.

Publisher, James A. Kuse
Editor/Ideals, Colleen Callahan Gonring
Associate Editor, Linda Robinson
Production Manager, Mark Brunner
Photographic Editor, Gerald Koser
Copy Editor, Barbara Nevid
Art Editor, Duane Weaver

September
Morn

Oh, happy bright September morn, how sweet and soft you are,
How very warm your morning sun, how bright your evening star;
Across the hilltops dawning breaks to start a full new day;
The world is fair, and nature smiles as autumn finds her way.

Oh, red and gold September morn with clear skies overhead
As summer slowly bids farewell and autumn smiles instead,
How gentle is the sighing breeze as treetops turn to gold
And, somewhere in the distance clear, an autumn story's told.

Oh, kissed with dew September morn, you've brought my heart a thrill;
Your laughter rings in sweet delight on every golden hill.
The roses bloom in softest hues though leaves are tumbling down;
There's gorgeous beauty unsurpassed in country and in town.

Oh, precious dear September morn, so melancholy now,
The green has changed to red and gold on every windswept bough.
Old Mother Nature reaches forth to glorify her earth.
Oh, heavenly September morn, how can we judge your worth?

Garnett Ann Schultz

Autumn Remembered

"Mama, is summer done and gone so soon?" I remember well the answer that she gave.

"Child, it isn't meant to last forever. Yes, I believe another summer's passed."

Rosy apples fell from the trees—some we ate, some just rotted, and some we threw away when the leaves fell and the trees stood naked.

Friendly birds seemed to vanish in a day.

Standing before a half-closed window, I'd shiver in my flannel nightgown, listening to the sounds in the heart of a night, watching countless silhouettes of flocks in flight crossing the broad expanse of the flaming, dying harvest moon.

I remember the smell of logs piled high against the woodshed and kindling filling all the bins. I remember feeling sad when I had to go to bed aware of cold, strange new winds nestling in the tree branches outside my room.

Dreadful state of affairs—getting up in the dark of mornings, having to go to bed too soon, wishing somebody could do something about this rapid time of dying, coming too fast.

Autumn danced in like a fairy queen, touching her wand ever so lightly over the farm, changing everything, creeping along in a graceful, quiet, assured way, sweeping the pathways clean that led to winter's door.

Leaves twisted, turning upon the trees, writhing a few rain-beaten days, and fell to earth to whisper no more.

Jump ropes slapped the earth with a twanging sound.

There was the joy of finding soft fur-lined rabbit nests and watching the raccoon carrying her babies by the nape of their little necks and a possum carrying her newborn in her warm pouch.

Barn bats, hidden under the eaves bedded upside down, stirred and stretched their wings, opened sleepy eyes. Squirrels busied themselves hiding precious nuts. Beavers buried green logs and twigs. Chipmunks carried grain and seeds. Honeybees sealed up their houses, saving all that nice honey until spring. Snails drew up in their shells.

There were screech owls wailing. I saw the wild ducks flying home, scarecrows standing lonely in the fields, and mother hens spreading their wings to hide their near-grown chicks from the hawks circling overhead.

Honeysuckle leaves lost their snap when I sucked them against my teeth. Mama's morning glories faded, leaving soft brown balls of seed that she gathered up to store away. There was goldenrod over the fields, and there was ragweed that made me sneeze.

Each night got longer, and there was time for roasting goobers, forgetting sweet magnolia smells, and everyone drawing closer together.

I remember listening to the tall stories Papa would tell and the clear sound of Mama's singing as she milked the cows down in the barn.

I remember the smell of mincemeat in the skillet, sugary aromas in every room, and spicy cookies filling the crocks.

I remember the first fire Mama made in the big old fireplace every autumn while the dogs slept peacefully on the hearth and the cats curled up … purring … sleeping but aware. The fire felt good on all sides of you.

I remember Papa mending the footlog over the creek, getting it ready for us to cross on our way to school.

I remember thinking, as slowly the thought permeated, "Why, winter won't be so bad!" I'd forgotten all the fun we had.

Steven-Adele Morley

Autumn

Roadsides lined with goldenrod
And trees of flaming hue,
Fruits and nuts all gathered in,
The face of earth is new.
The crisp cool air of morning,
Indicative of fall,
Paints pictures of contentment,
Splashed color over all.
Happy, cozy time of year
When food is garnered in,
Then color rules the roadside,
And stores are in the bin.

Mary A. Barnard

Gertrude Bryson Holman

Gertrude Bryson Holman has always enjoyed living in the country for its "spaciousness, serenity and natural beauty." She remembers numerous pleasant experiences during her childhood on a farm in western Texas and refers to these memories in many of her writings, including a column in her hometown newspaper. As a young girl and throughout her life, Mrs. Holman was afflicted with a heart condition which never adversely affected her naturally caring and cheerful disposition. A mother of five children, Gertrude Holman taught elementary school for many years—her first school being a one-room house with only seven pupils. She describes her dedicated years of teaching as being challenging and rewarding. In one of her books *Seasoned with Salt,* which contains her personal insights and reflections on life, she writes, "I have learned to accept the seasons as they come, with my work and dreams going hand in hand."

Autumn

The summer sun is now quite mellow,
And leaves have turned to brown and yellow.
Golden pumpkins ripen on the vine
And bring such tasty pies to mind.

The wild geese with their honking cry
Go southward as they soar on high,
While Nature with a lavish hand
Spreads grandeur throughout the land.

Autumn's Benediction

The trees uplift their arms in prayer
To bless each leaflet hanging there
Before they leave the mother tree
To swirl and dance so merrily.

The leaves have gathered tints of flowers,
The glories of the sunset hours;
And now they scatter gifts of gold
According to the customs old.

Enchantment fills the evening air;
The trees renounce all ills and care.
With inner peace and humble pride,
I turn to the comfort of my fireside.

Autumn Is Coming

The night wind whispers to the trees
That autumn season's on the way.
There's coolness in the fresh night air;
November weather's here to stay.

The rusty leaves begin to stir;
The garden flowers brown silently
As bulbs mature and tops fall down,
Prepared for frost that's yet to be.

The cricket's song is sad and low;
Strange birds flit in the golden sun;
The rumor's going from tree to tree
That summer's burning heat is done.

November stays the hand of time—
A pause between the summer's heat
And winter's frosty searing cold.
These golden autumn days we greet!

Autumn Gold

The day is born with golden sun
Diffused by God's own lavish hand;
The meadows, hills, and valleys wide
Become a blessed, golden land.

The sunset crowns the day with gold
Which soon gives way to stars' bright eyes;
The pale moon pauses on her way
To climb the stairway to the skies.

There's golden sand and sheaves of grain
And gold in groves of cottonwood trees;
Metallic gold and jeweled stones
Cannot compare with such as these.

There's gold in the flowers that bloom,
The sunflowers bright and goldenrod,
The golden notes of birds that sing—
All touched by the hand of God.

Autumn in the Country

As Autumn walks across the land,
The hills are bathed in gold.
The gnarled old oak with foliage dark,
Beside the sumac bold,
Sheds hallowed splendor far and wide
At lovely Autumn's feet.
The sheen of sunshine on the lake
Brings warmth to my retreat.

A breath of wind stirred up the leaves
Which rustled on the ground.
Such heavenly tranquillity
This moment I have found.
I felt that Time was standing still;
The sky and lake and all
The trees were wayside chapels—
Such beauty in the fall!

Signs of Autumn

There is a hint of gold among the trees;
A touch of nippy frost is in the air.
The squirrels are hoarding nuts for winter days;
They scurry round and hide them with great care.

I hear the plaintive coo of a mourning dove
And share the cardinal's song of praise.
The wild geese honk as they fly swift and low;
I'm sure this is a sign of autumn days.

The wooded hills hold grandeur for us all,
And mums are flashing colors far and near.
All these are telling us the latest news
That golden, mellow autumn days are here.

Tender Are the Leaves

After months of summertime,
Falling leaves begin to shine;
Friendly colors dance with grace,
Shining moments of happy lace.

Playful angels smile with glee,
Chasing shadows so joyfully;
Flowing brooks join in fun
Where the breezes and fishes run.

Near the voice of harvesttime,
Garnished bells begin to chime;
A chaliced heart where bluebirds call
Creates the joy of a waterfall.

Can I doubt that God exists
When I see scenes like this?
Now I bow beneath the trees
Beside the artist upon my knees.

Wayne B. Dayton

Suddenly— September!

Just overnight the goldenrod
Puts on its dusty golden plumes,
And from the sun-dried milkweed pods
Whirl fairies midst frost-flower blooms.
Beside the fence of weathered gray,
Queen Anne has spread her lace to dry.
The trees flaunt patchwork gaudy, gay,
And woodsmoke spirals toward the sky.
The sumac glows; the candle trees
Lift golden tapers; wood-vines blush.
There's sudden whisperings of the leaves
When night-winds sigh through evening's hush.
Who saw the Summer as she left
Tiptoeing through the moonlit frost?
Who heard her crying as, bereft,
She wandered lonely, chilled and lost?
For suddenly September comes,
Her banners bold with Autumn gleams,
To heralding of partridge drums,
And Summer leaves but echoed dreams.

Ruth B. Field

Monarch Butterflies

No leaded windows glow in distant France
More clear than these wings of monarch butterflies
Here on the tilted branch of chrysanthemum,
A second flowering, unforetold,
Burnished topaz lined with antique gold!

Brief as autumn's slanted sun, they come,
Sipping the nectar of the daisyed blooms.
Opening, enfolding the fruited air, fragile
Panels of color borne from valleys spired
With Gothic cathedrals. Briefly I enfold
In the window of my memory this gold.

Marjorie A. Elliott

Flames of Autumn

Burn brightly, flames of autumn.
Let scarlet sumac blaze
And poplars flame with golden fire
These gleaming autumn days.

Let maples' ruby sweep of flame,
The elm trees' glowing gold
And garnet oak tree radiance
Bring warmth to days grown cold.

Burn brightly, flames of autumn.
A grateful heart remembers
The lambent beauty of your fires
Long after they are embers.

Gail Brook Burket

Siesta

The final flowering
Of September's garden glory
Is steeped in languor.

Cottages,
Flanked with bright color,
Doze in the sun.

Hints of autumn tinge
The deepening russet gold
Of evening sunsets.

E. Cole Ingle

Earth's Bright Pageantry

The hills are full of color;
Now sumacs are ablaze
While maples flame, and sassafras,
These vivid autumn days.

The hickories are golden,
The poplars golden, too;
The beech is burnished copper,
The elms, a russet hue.

There's glory in each hollow;
The hills in glory stand.
A pageantry of color
Has swept across the land.

Edith Shaw Butler

September

Blue and gold of spring,
Gathered glow of summer brightness
Blending
Into tawny spice-scented zinnias,
Flaming in aster and chrysanthemum;

We have waited
For this carnival of flowers.
Green is fading.
Let it go. We will remember
This kaleidoscope of autumn hours.

Marjorie Bertram Smith

It's Autumn

There's a harvest moon a'shining
Above each country lane,
And chill winds of the evening
Call through the leaves again.

The clustered grapes a'hanging
From the arbor vine
Breathe out an invitation
To this grateful heart of mine.

There's a scent of leaf-smoke drifting
Sweet and pungent on the air;
White and gold chrysanthemums
Are nodding everywhere.

Out on the hills and meadows,
Wherever one may wander,
We'll find the plumes of goldenrod
With untold wealth to squander.

Lucille Crumley

Indian Summer
Jay H. Meyers

Indian summer, fickle lady,
With your frock of many hues,
Gardens bright with autumn flowers,
Late bees sipping nectar brews;

Colors cast by nature's paintbrush—
Browns, greens, and scarlets bright—
Dressing all the hills and valleys,
Jack Frost changing them each night;

Silver dew on morning meadow,
Early birdcalls growing still,
Silken webs are gently floating
Through the poplars on the hill.

Golden pumpkins, apples glowing
In the orchard's fragrant lane,
Cider barrels are overflowing,
Grasses brown on hill and plain;

Oh, fair and fickle lady,
Warm and bright your gay attire
Bringing happy autumn evenings
Spent with loved ones by the fire.

Roadside Stands in September

Roadside stands in the country
In the month of September
Are a kaleidoscope of color—
Truly something to remember.

There are heaps of orange pumpkins;
The apples are ruby red;
Chrysanthemums flaunt golden petals
Before they finally shed.

Onions are pearllike in beauty;
There are chestnuts for roasting
On winter days ahead when lads
On their sleds are coasting.

See the bright sprays of bittersweet;
There is multihued Indian corn, too;
And grapes from nearby vineyards
That add a purplish blue.

When we visit the roadside stands
In the burnished month of September,
We come away loaded with treasure
And with pleasantries to remember!

Earle J. Grant

Autumn Evening

What magic there is in the wand
Which autumn wields
When it pours its stream of gold
On the harvest fields:
A loveliness tinting all
That shines to the eyes,
With purple curtains of haze
Let down from the skies;
The maples with flaming banners
In every wood,
The cornstalks like ranks
Of a rustic brotherhood;
The barns all bursting with grain
As the apples fall,
And a wondrous peace
Seems somehow part of it all.
There are rainbow colors
Mirrored in placid streams,
And earth seems hushed
To a music of whispers and dreams.
The bees are filling their hives
With a dusty gold,
And the heart is filled
With more than a heart can hold.

Vincent Godfrey Burns

It's Hayride Time Tonight

The pumpkins are a radiant orange;
The moon is full and bright;
It's time to gather one and all
For hayride time tonight.

The air is crisp and nippy now;
The leaves are on the ground,
So put on scarves and mittens when
The hayrack comes around.

It is a time for fellowship
And spirits gay and light.
The hay is ready on the racks
For hayride fun tonight.

We'll travel through the countryside
And thrill to autumn's touch,
So hitch the horses, and we're off
For times we love so much.

Craig E. Sathoff

October

The frosts of October are white on the grass,
The meadows and fields turning brown;
The leaves of the maples, in showers of gold,
Drift silently, steadily down.

Against the gray wall the pale asters are massed
Like clusters of stars, blue and white;
Over all is a shimmering, glimmering haze
Pierced through with gold arrows of light.

Afar on the hill burn the sumac's deep fires,
And goldenrod waves far and near;
For golden October's abroad in the land—
Most beautiful month of the year.

Horace A. Roberts

See lovely autumn's golden days
And hillsides draped in purple haze,
The silhouettes of barren trees
Accenting those still filled with leaves,

Autumn Beauty

Evelyn Hawkins Guthrie

Green, scarlet, yellow, every hue
Against a sky of cobalt blue,
High hedges fringed with lacy weed
Where Robin Redbreast comes to feed,

A split-rail fence, time-weathered gray,
The perfect setting for the play
Of nature at her very best
Before the earth must take its rest

To sleep throughout long winter's reign
Till south wind wakens earth again
To beauty only nature knows,
Another blessing God bestows.

Autumn

Each of the seasons has its own special flavor.
Summer's bountiful and ever-changing floral display
turns to both the muteness and vibrancy of fall
as nature flings her colors across the landscape
without regard to what went before.

A stroll through a landscape as sizzling as
an artist's palette reveals the most lavish color,
the shadings of which are far beyond
the ability of the eye to catalog.

Every step discloses some unexpected pleasure.
The bucolic atmosphere of a quiet village,
rich in the lore and tradition of its ancestry,
is suddenly festive in its extraordinary
Ferris wheel of color.

Wide tree-lined streets are framed in a bower of pageantry,
and crisp leaves underfoot resemble
the splendorous patterns in a great Persian rug.
Fall's magnificent burst of beauty is everywhere.

Virginia Funk

Payment

My neighbor just laughs as she watches me raking,
For the leaves on my lawn came straight from her tree.
She offered to help, and I was quite tempted,
But declined when I realized I owed her this fee.

For her tree gave me shade all through the summer
And cooled off my lawn in the heat of the day.
My tag sale was broadcast from one of its branches,
And my kids had a place to climb and to play.

Begrudge her this time (not to mention the blisters)?
Oh, no! I consider it time so well spent.
I can't own this tree; it belongs to my neighbor,
But by raking her leaves, at least I can rent.

                                        Eileen Hession

These

I shall remember these this autumn day:
The silken whir of wings outside my door,
Bright pools of autumn sunlight on the floor,
A flaunting maple's gold and crimson sheen,
A towering pine tree with its fadeless green,
A stately goldenrod with tall slim grace,
A garden spider's thin and brown-spun lace,
A row of golden pumpkins on the earth,
A child's impulsive laugh of wholesome mirth,
Wild grapes that shimmer in a leaf-strewn field,
The perfume roses of late summer yield,
The gentian with purple head so meek,
And lovely words I hear you softly speak.

William Arnette Wofford

Autumn Tapestry

Special Thoughts About Autumn

Mark the wreath about my head—
Wreath of richest flowers;
I am Autumn, and I bring
Mildest, happiest hours;
In my hand a goblet see,
Which the grape juice holds;
Corn and grain and precious fruits,
Autumn's arm enfolds.

Emily Carter

The meadows belong to the summer
Where the grain and the grasses grow tall,
But the hills, bathed in breathtaking beauty,
Can only belong to the fall.

Nadine Brothers Lybarger

The first frost
Turns the ferns
To rust,
Departing
In a golden dust,
And through the trees
The autumn sun
Informs the leaves
That summer's done.

John Fenton Lowry

The flaming trees have quickly laid
A gala carpet all around,
For Autumn's golden-sandaled feet
Must never dance on barren ground.

Sarah Mizelle Morgan

Frost set the leaves to quaking;
Sap hurried to the roots;
And Autumn came out walking
In his golden boots.

June Masters Bacher

There's something about
A crisp fall day
To remind us that God
Is planning His way
To take the warmth
And sunshine away
But leave autumn's glow
To brighten our way.

Sallie Bristow

Bring the glory of autumn into our souls,
The peace of God to our hearts.
We bow our heads in reverent grace
For the blessings this season imparts.

Vera Stahly

Now that autumn days are here
And leaves are falling one by one,
The trees prepare a coverlet
For weary Earth, whose work is done;
For she must slumber till the dawn
That brings the sun of springtime morn.

Georgia Day Sherwood

Autumn prays in smoky gray;
Spirals rise until
Their silver shadows fade away
Beyond the golden hill.

Elisabeth A. Toland Currie

Where in all the world is there
A ballet floating through the air
As lovely as the dancing leaves of autumn?

Pamela Vaull Starr

Chrysanthemums are rioting
Against the garden wall,
A mass of flaming color
Growing sturdily and tall.

Their reds and pinks and yellows,
Their russets and their gold,
Their snowdrop white, their lavender
Just deepen with the cold.

And so, when I feel sorrowful
That spring has turned to fall,
I just look at chrysanthemums
Against the garden wall.

Margery Burke Burrowes

Oh, how I love an October day
When I can mingle work with play,
Raking leaves in the warm sunrays,
Storing up memories for wintry days.

Marjorie Martin

White ghosts screech
as witches ride
high above the countryside.

On backyard walls
black cats preen.
Once again it's Halloween.

Maxine Bell

The hawthorn bloomed in April,
A mountain-high bouquet—
The pinks and whites of springtime—
Then petals blew away.

And now it is October
When breath is steamed with cold,
And hawthorn in the hollow
Blooms out in magic gold.

June Masters Bacher

Say good-bye to summer now;
Leaves are turning on the bough.

Grain has ripened in the field;
Orchards offer up their yield.

Gold and russet days are here
For the harvest of the year.

Edith Shaw Butler

October rushes busily
Rolling up her sleeves,
Shaking out her carpets,
Brushing down her leaves,
Gathering in her harvests,
Making crannies tight,
Preparing beds for winter,
Turning down the light.

Emily Carey Alleman

Autumn Reflections

The leaves are turning jewel-shades,
And cars in endless, long parades
Converge upon each lakeside town
To view this beauty of renown.

There is no pen which can describe
Such loveliness, nor any scribe
Can show with words the majesty
With which God beautifies each tree.

One's eyes cannot believe the sight
Of jeweled trees which overnight
Have taken on such kingly garb,
From towering oak to lowly barb,

The skies are a deep, burning blue
Accenting every jeweled hue
Of scarlet sumac and ruby red
Which flames in maples overhead.

Like crystal mirrors, deep and still,
The lakes reflect each jeweled hill
That rings this land with quiet grace
And beauty in its form and face.

The air is pungent with the scent
That autumn brings, and deep content
Floods through the hearts of all who share
This autumn-land beyond compare!

Dorothy L. Black

Magic

I love the way that Autumn trims a town,
   September-kissed,
With russet lace and furbelows of brown
   And violet mist.

I love the way her hands can touch a tree
   And leave a trace
Of gold dust and of scarlet witchery
   Upon its face;
The wild geese flying high that break the hush
   Of early dawn,
The sound of restless, singing winds that brush
   Across the lawn.

I love the way that Autumn, wild and sweet,
   Can weave a touch of magic in each street.

Catherine E. Berry

Melancholy Season?

Season of sadness?
Surely not the fall,
When October dances
In a gypsy shawl,
When sumac fires the hillside,
When geese vagabond the sky,
When blue and gold sapphire the air
And woodsmoke spirals high,
When frost sprinkles red on all the trees
And thistledown floats lightly in the breeze,
When college opens and gaiety is over all.
Is the melancholy season in the fall?

Stella Craft Tremble

Autumn in Your Hand

Hal Borland

A tree in autumn is a lovely sight. One tree alone can concentrate the beauty of a whole woodland, leaf by leaf and branch by branch, as one flower can give the essence of a whole garden. The beauty of the turning woods is not alone in the scarlet of a maple grove or the sun-gold glow of a hillside stand of beeches. It is in the subtle change that creeps along the leaves themselves, from point to point and vein to vein. A woodland in full color is awesome as a forest fire, in magnitude at least; but a single tree is like a dancing tongue of flame to warm the heart.

Watch even a single branch outside a certain window, and you are watching the color of change. One morning there is a spot of yellow on a certain leaf, yellow which has not yet quite achieved the glow of gold. Another day and that glow may be there. It spreads. The spot becomes a splash of gold, edged perhaps with a thin line of scarlet. It creeps down the leaf between the veins, and then across the veins; and the scarlet edging widens into a band and then a border. Meanwhile other leaves have begun to turn, some to gold, some to dull bronze, some to blood-red beauty. All on the same branch as full of color as the whole woodland.

Thus comes autumn, leaf by leaf and tree by tree; thus the woods become a hooked rug flung across the hills with all its folds and all its colors as they came to hand. But pause beside one tree and look, and you can see autumn on all the hills. Pick up one leaf of those already cast adrift and you hold autumn in your hand.

Beautiful Mountains

How beautiful the mountains are
As Autumn days unfold,
When great oak leaves are turning red
And maple leaves to gold,

The peacefulness of wooded hills
Where singing creeks run free
When larks and robins on the wing
Add their sweet melody,

How beautiful the distant peaks,
Each wreathed in purple haze,
From drifting smoke of phantom fires
On Indian summer days,

Through long cathedrals, vaulted high,
Made by the arching trees—
To kneel there on a carpet bright
Of painted Autumn leaves.

How beautiful their sunsets are
And twilight's afterglow
When gold sunfires send streamers high
As shadows come and go.

How beautiful the mountains are
From dawns to sunsets rare
When Autumn walks the hills and vales
With oak leaves in her hair.

Florence Howery Roddy

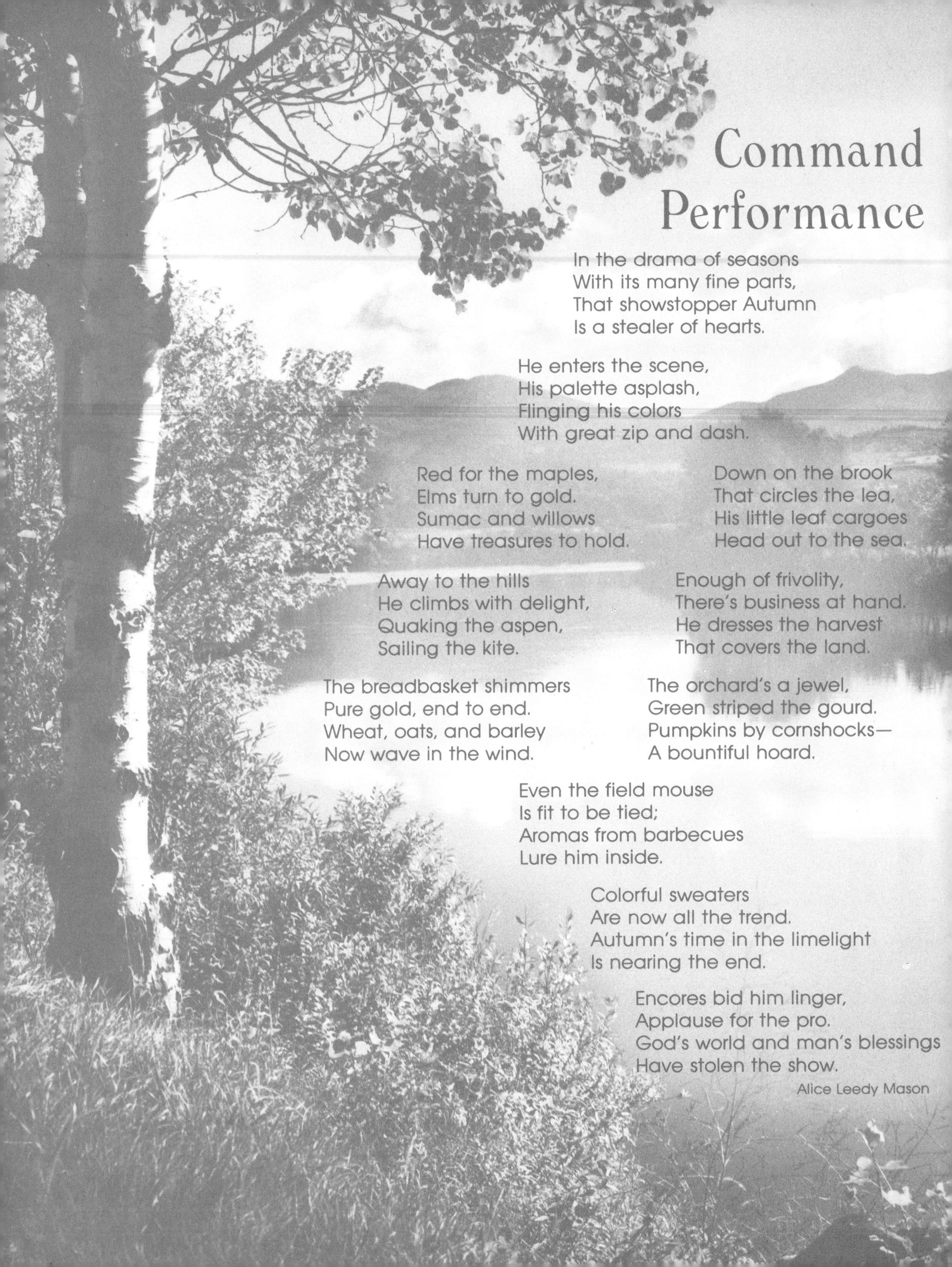

Command Performance

In the drama of seasons
With its many fine parts,
That showstopper Autumn
Is a stealer of hearts.

He enters the scene,
His palette asplash,
Flinging his colors
With great zip and dash.

Red for the maples,
Elms turn to gold.
Sumac and willows
Have treasures to hold.

Down on the brook
That circles the lea,
His little leaf cargoes
Head out to the sea.

Away to the hills
He climbs with delight,
Quaking the aspen,
Sailing the kite.

Enough of frivolity,
There's business at hand.
He dresses the harvest
That covers the land.

The breadbasket shimmers
Pure gold, end to end.
Wheat, oats, and barley
Now wave in the wind.

The orchard's a jewel,
Green striped the gourd.
Pumpkins by cornshocks—
A bountiful hoard.

Even the field mouse
Is fit to be tied;
Aromas from barbecues
Lure him inside.

Colorful sweaters
Are now all the trend.
Autumn's time in the limelight
Is nearing the end.

Encores bid him linger,
Applause for the pro.
God's world and man's blessings
Have stolen the show.

Alice Leedy Mason

October Rain

Last night it came into our town
On quiet, slippered feet.
We could scarcely hear it falling
On the roof or in the street.

It dripped so very softly
From the porches and the eaves
That we almost had the feeling
That 'twas rustling autumn leaves.

It bathed the lawn refreshingly;
It touched the windowpane;
It kissed the city's dusty face—
Then tiptoed out again.

Elsie DeRuiter

Borne by the Breeze

How lively is autumn when the leaves flit by,
Tracing a crimson path through the azure sky,
Heaping their gold in the poplar's shade,
Tumbling and tripping over lawns yellow jade.

Wafted away from their lofty sphere
By a gust or a flurry that suddenly appears,
They drift on the strength of a passing breeze,
Onward and downward away from their trees,

Tumbling and twirling, in their moments of glee,
To the earth where they trip fetterless and free,
Blending their shades of amber, crimson and gold,
Matting the ground with a patchwork rich to behold!

What an autumnal delight to shuffle along
Nudged by a breeze and soothed by a song—
A song that is whispered by fluttering leaves,
Rustling and tumbling wherever they please!

Joy Belle Burgess

From Small Beginnings

A tiny acorn doing chin-ups on a limb high in the top of an old oak tree was snatched on the whim of a playful breeze and dropped to the ground below. The little acorn held his breath and squeezed his eyes shut tight till he landed with an almost imperceptible thud on the soft forest floor. Nestling into the warm earth under a blanket of leaves, he surveyed with interest his newfound world of giants. But the little acorn wasn't afraid—he was possessed by a sense of his own destiny.

Most of the old-timers took scant notice of the newcomer, if, indeed, they were aware of his existence at all. A few, however, shot contemptuous glances at him, and a tall, slender pine languidly waved a branch in his direction and looked at her unkempt companion, who wept incessantly because her long, unruly locks kept trailing in the brook at her feet.

"There, there, Willow dear. Don't go on so. If you think you've got problems, just look at that scrawny little upstart over there. It's plain to see he'll never amount to much!"

The little acorn just smiled to himself and snuggled down deeper into his cozy nest, and soon he fell asleep.

While he slept, the soft spring rains came and crooned a soothing lullaby overhead, as the gentle breezes strummed an accompaniment on the uppermost branches. Then one day a passing earthworm brushed against the little acorn and jarred him into wakefulness. He yawned and stretched, then stretched again so hard that he burst right out of himself, sending a tiny green shoot upward through the soil.

"So this is what it feels like to be a tree," the little acorn thought, noting that his broken shell made him more vulnerable to his surroundings. "This growing up is not all it's cracked up to be."

But grow he did. And the taller he grew, the farther down into the earth he pushed his roots and the harder he dug in. Soon he had carved out a place for himself among the other trees of the forest.

Still, it wasn't easy, even then. He had his

good times and his bad times. There were verdant spring seasons when the air was heavy with the fragrance of life and the songs of the birds echoed from the forest walls. There were warm summer days when chattering squirrels scampered through his branches laying up their stores for the coming months; but there were also frosty autumn nights when he shivered so hard he shed all his leaves so that, when the snows came, he implored the drifting flakes to winter on his exposed limbs and cover his nakedness.

One year an outlaw wind invaded the tranquillity of the forest, snapping limbs and branches at random and even uprooting whole trees in some instances. Though the oak tree stood his ground, when the wind had at last spent its fury, the weary tree ached and groaned in every fiber of his being.

Another time a tropical rain swept inland across the plains from the ocean beyond and lingered over the forest for days. Once the clouds had finally emptied themselves of their watery burden, the little brook spread out of its banks, its swollen form sprawled among the trees. Thoroughly wet and uncomfortable, the miserable oak shook himself time and again, sending showers of droplets down on the hapless creatures that had gathered to seek refuge among his gnarled roots.

Then came the day when a sudden summer storm reached down a fiery finger of lightning and deftly severed every limb halfway down one side of his mighty trunk. Yet, even as the blue smoke curled heavenward, the oak tree did not flinch. If anything, he stood taller and prouder than ever, as if in arrogant defiance of the elements.

Having withstood the onslaught of wind and rain and his baptism of fire, the noble oak tree was allowed to live out his final years in peace, attaining a ripe old age and establishing himself as the patriarch of the forest, which he had helped to populate. By now he had himself lost track of the number of young trees he had fathered.

As he reminisced, he was momentarily distracted by the antics of his youngest, a lively little fellow who was constantly in motion. As the oak tree watched, the little acorn lost his grip on the twig from which he was swinging

and plummeted to the forest floor. For the most part, the incident went unnoticed by the old oak's neighbors, except for one honey-voiced magnolia, who lifted a pale blossom toward a stately cottonwood standing nearby.

"Woody darlin'," she drawled, "isn't that just the funniest thing? I do believe that little acorn actually turned loose on purpose! Whatever for, do you suppose? Surely he doesn't fancy himself a tree!"

But the old oak tree chuckled into his flowing gray beard of Spanish moss, for he remembered what it was like to be an acorn.

And the little acorn just smiled to himself and snuggled down deeper into the warm earth, and soon he fell asleep.   Patsy Ray

Here's October

You can hear October walking
Through the heaps of fallen leaves;
You can hear October talking
In the wind among the trees.

And her voice is gaily ringing
All along the rolling hills
And her lilting laughter singing
From the brooks and little rills.

You can see October dancing
On the water's sparkling crest,
And you're thinking "here's October,
And I love October best."

Clasp her hand and ramble with her
All along the hills and dales;
Keep the memory of her sunshine
Through the winter's chilly gales.

See the lovely autumn season
Holding out her treasure chest,
And be glad for every reason
That you love October best.

Ada M. McCalvy

Stronghold
Julia Lott

These are the tokens of the passing year:
That bittersweet, epitome of fall,
Bursts orange red; the air is honey-clear,
And trees are drooping with a blackbird pall.
Bright pumpkins, gleaming on the fodder shocks;
The lengthened shadows and the shortened day;
Wild geese and mallards, flying high in flocks;
The light of bonfires; meadows turning gray;
Blue morning glories that defy the frost
And gorgeous leaves that make the woodlands burn
With color are the tokens and the lost.
These are the passing things. In need we turn
To seeds and bulbs and deeply rooted trees;
As in the winters past, we trust in these.

Bittersweet
Ruth Ricker Pappas

As wintertime approaches and all the world looks bare,
Our eyes turn toward the bittersweet with a very quizzical stare.
All other growing things have left us long ago,
But here's the flaming bittersweet, its beauty all aglow.
We pass it by in summer, with its leaves of waxy green,
Just another climbing vine where birds can sit and preen.
But suddenly when gardens die and leaves come falling down,
We look back at the bittersweet in its dazzling orange gown.
The leaves we once admired have all fallen to the ground,
And there, in great resplendency, are berries firm and round.
We turn our eyes in admiration at the beauty which we see
And wonder how this miracle ever came to be.
Flocks of birds descend upon it for a tidbit now and then,
The sparrow and the chickadee, the blue jay and the wren;
So open wide your eyes and see God's beauty all around,
And be thankful that on earth such wonders do abound.

Autumn

Isabelle Lane Partise

Autumn romps through dusty woods
And fingerpaints the trees,
Then casts a mist of diamond dust
To frost the passing breeze.

Autumn breathes on windowpanes
And writes her name in lace,
Then tiptoes over rigid grass
To touch a rosy face.

Autumn creeps neath patchwork quilt
And tucks it tight to chin.
So tired, she sleeps on fallen leaves,
Lulled by the wild gale's din.

Autumn rests, her labors done,
Washed clean by icy rain.
She smoothes the snow folds and sleeps
Neath Winter's counterpane.

Frost Pictures

Edna Jaques

Frost pictures on the window,
How they glow for my delight!
An artist with a silver brush
Had made them in the night.
He left an etching frail as lace
Of ferns and fairy things,
A tiny mountain capped with snow,
A bird with shining wings.

And when the sun came up at last
To rout the frosty mist,
He turned them all to ruby red
With fans of amethyst,
A painting wrought in golden fire
That smote the heart of me—
A masterpiece of jewels set
In silver filigree.

Columbus
the Dauntless

Men said the earth was flat,
  A square by angles bound,
But one courageous soul resolved
  To prove our planet round.

Men scoffed and ridiculed
  And laughed his plan to scorn.
His pleadings met derision's taunt
  And gibes from morn to morn.

But vision vaults blockades;
  Conviction conquers foes.
Naught is achieved without a will
  To thwart a dreamer's woes.

Because of his persistence,
  Tenacity and tact,
A Spanish queen, her faith bestirred,
  Provided funds he lacked.

Ere long, with ships and hearty men,
  With gaze far out to sea,
Columbus challenged westward waves
  To chance catastrophe.

But faith begets achievement,
  And vision precedes fact;
O'er bounding waves and mutinous men
  He gained the proof that lacked.

We hail thee, Friend Columbus!
  In honor, not in jest,
For history were sad at best
  Without thy daring quest.

John B. Peterson

The Beauty of the Farm

There's so much lasting beauty on the farm
Among the common things.
We cannot name the countless things
Upon a farm that one day brings—
The cows that stand beneath the trees,
Or wind through the gate at night;
The bedded sheep or piglets small,
The rooster crowing at daylight;
And when in spring the flowers bloom,
Bluebonnets paint the hillside bare
And sturdy daisies crowd the path
And clover scents the air.

In summertime when fruit is ripe
And all the garden's at its best.
We can and freeze and store our food
And know that country life is best.
But when the Autumn paints the scene
In crimson banners, bronze and gold,
We feel a lasting beauty then—
Almost too much a heart can hold.
My cottage window frames a scene
On any sunny winter day,
The tapestry of field and lake
So fair they steal my breath away.

Gertrude Bryson Holman

Finding the Great Pumpkin

Martin Hintz

Linus, of Peanuts comic-strip fame, isn't the only one who excitedly waits for harvesttime. The arrival of the Great Pumpkin has just as much import in our house as well. The tension builds in direct relationship to the changing shades of the oaks in the park across the street. Honking geese, on their frosty skyway south, don't bring messages of any impending winter storm—at least not to our home. Their autumn farewell simply means that it's time to head for the country to search out the jumboest, the greatest giant-economy size cucurbita pepo ever grown (that means a big pumpkin) ... a tall order, indeed! (Pumpkins come in about fifty varieties, ranging from midgets to mammoths, from sugary, meaty pie types to the rugged jack-o'-lantern.)

Visions of vast fields overflowing with the dull golden globes dance through the dreams of our three children. Pumpkins the size of houses are out there, somewhere, just awaiting the plucking, the carving, and the pie making. Every year it's the same. Every fall, a major expedition must be mounted with all the preparation of a long safari into the African veld.

This pumpkin hunting is serious, all right. It's our personal challenge to beat the records of previous quests—quests that seem to blossom with more details in each recounting.

"Remember that one we had last year? Dad almost had to have a tractor scoop to load it into the trunk," spurts Dan with the exaggerated enthusiasm of a ten year old. "I found 'fifty that were the biggest," brags seven-year-old Steve. Kate, at four, isn't quite the veteran hunter like her brothers but still has some things to add. "I'm gonna find the bestest one ever," she claims, always the optimist.

For weeks—even as winds turn chilly, gray clouds scud angrily across the horizon, and leaves whip and dance across the road—the questions come from the small people. When do we go? Can we go today? Aw, come on, the good pumpkins will all be gone! Halloween is only four weeks away! What about the pies?

When it's finally time to select pumpkins, everyone eagerly gets into the car for the excursion.

As we drive, the roadside stands we see have to pass a test before we can stop for a spot check. They must be filled to overflowing with gourds and goodies, literally brimming to the bursting point with pattypan, crookneck and hybrid summer squashes, pumpkin varieties called Funny Face and Spirit, freshly picked apples and jugs of cider, multicolored Indian corn, and baskets of nuts.

Never, absolutely never, do we snatch up what seems to be the first delightfully round, perfectly formed pumpkin we see. Perfection is only a mind state anyway. The next place down the line might have a pumpkin that's a bit bigger, a fraction fruitier. This search takes a full Saturday or Sunday afternoon of walking, thumping, lifting, comparing, and questioning before a wise choice can be made.

We wander far off the major roads, chugging over the hilly landscape, pausing at farmsites with hand-lettered signs that say "Pumpkins for Sale." The best deals can be made with youthful entrepreneurs who claim that their prices are lower and their pumpkins are better than all others. It's hard to resist sales talks like that. So usually we relent and stash away a couple of fifteen-pounders as extras for the side windows of our house.

It's the pumpkin farms, however, that really attract our attention. These are the pampering places that nurture grand champions with great care. These meccas of fruitdom are sought eagerly. The pick-your-own places offer the widest selection, even if it means wandering through muddy fields.

Everyone heads for the tangle of vines webbing their way across the remains of the

harvested corn. Tucked among the withered leaves are the truly monstrous pumpkins that conform to most of the criteria the family has for size, color, shape, and texture. These are the ones too big to be removed by the farmer, so he leaves them for the city gleaner to haul away. This is a booted operation, with feet slopping through the mire and with fingers muddy from turning pumpkins over to check their undersides. Some of the best-looking pumpkins have soft underbellies, the result of sitting too long on the ground. Others, with all the glowing golden color we could desire, sound rotten inside, the thump of a mittened hand not echoing quite right. Seasons of experience give the dedicated pumpkin thumper practice in choosing correctly. This sometimes involves running from one end of the field to the other, answering the calls from each youngster that the pumpkin they've found beats all the rest.

If the price is right, as it usually is out here at the source, we are able to get several to rival state fair entries. Then we work, groaning, to lift or roll the prizes from field to car. The car dips lower with each trunk deposit. After the purchases are made, there may even be time for a jaunt in a tractor-pulled farm wagon around the back of the barn.

Tired bodies notwithstanding, the ride home must include a stop at a village ice-cream store for hot fudge sundaes all around and more chatter about the horribly scary faces that will soon grace each of the discoveries of that day.

Eventually, the selections will be displayed on the front porch railing with all their carved grimaces. The pumpkin seeds will be salted and oven dried, ready for munching by the handful. Window shades will be left open even when it becomes black outside and the time comes for tales of the headless horseman and other spirits of the season. By the flickering candlelight, this year's legends are born. So just wait, Great Pumpkin, the kids are already talking about future autumns ... when you'll be bigger than ever.

Apple-Picking Time

The sunshine is dreaming upon our hill
Where the orchard is mellow-sweet
With apples that glisten and gleam in the trees
And carpet the grass at my feet.

My father and I have baskets to fill
With the luscious fruit at its best,
And pure joy is mine up high in the boughs
Pursuing my glorious quest.

For apples that hide among the green leaves
Are brilliant as jewels on the stems,
And sweet are their charms that lure me on
To find the most radiant gems.

The apples still glisten and gleam in the trees
In the warmth of the drowsing sun,
And ever I'll search till I find my prize ...
The biggest and ripest one!

Joy Belle Burgess

My Name
Is
Jack

I was just the usual pumpkin
Till they found me on the farm.
Then they took me home and carved me—
Gave my face a special charm.
How my light glowed on the porch step!
How it flickered in the wind!
Ghosts and goblins smiled to see me.
When they called me Jack, I grinned.

David Lowell

By All These Signs I Knew

Today, upon a gold-crowned hill
I felt the first, faint frosty chill;
A leaf fell softly at my feet
Where mellow apples, musty sweet,
Perfumed the languid country air
And mingled with the scent of pear.

A redwing spurned his spring-built nest
And disappeared into the west;
Rose petals scattered on the ground
To cover up an earthy mound
That housed a sleepy, blinking toad,
While dust-whirls circled down the road.
Scarecrows, lately spruce and neat,
Drooped wearily in stubbled wheat.
By all these signs I knew, I knew,
Jack Frost was stirring Winter's brew.

Emily Carey Alleman

COLOR ART AND PHOTO CREDITS
(in order of appearance)

Front and back cover, Groton, Vermont, Freelance Photographers Guild; inside front cover, Craig Blouin; Roadside beauty near Sargentville, Maine, Colour Library International (USA) Limited; Fruits of harvest, Fred Sieb; First Indian Mission Church, Stockbridge, Massachusetts, Albert A. Trimels; Butterfly, Photo Graphics; Colorful contrasts in Adirondack State Park, New York, Ed Cooper; Cozy dwelling, Fred Sieb; Splash of color, Alpha Photo Associates; Country church near Waupaca, Wisconsin, Ken Dequaine; Autumn treasures, Alpha Photo Associates; Goldenrod, Gerald Koser; Rustic Wick House near Morristown, New Jersey, Alpha Photo Associates; Tree-lined highway near Kearsarge, New Hampshire, Fred Sieb; Autumn bike ride, Bob Taylor; Shadow Lake, Waupaca, Wisconsin, Ken Dequaine; Washington Vine Maple leaves, Cascade Mountains, Ed Cooper; Peaceful lake, Fred Sieb; Forest floor near Stratton Lake, Waupaca, Wisconsin, Ken Dequaine; Rogue River, Rogue River National Forest, Oregon, Josef Muench; Frost picture, Surrey, England, Colour Library International (USA) Limited; Landing of Columbus, Ed Lambert; Autumn reflection, H. Armstrong Roberts; Apples near Egg Harbor, Door County, Wisconsin, Ken Dequaine; Bountiful harvest, Fred Sieb; Halloween fun, Fred Sieb; Trick or treat, H. Armstrong Roberts; inside back cover, Fred Sieb.

ACKNOWLEDGMENTS

BY ALL THESE SIGNS I KNEW and WHEN SUMMER COMES (October rushes busily . . .) by Emily Carey Alleman. From her book: THE GYPSY HEART, Copyright © 1957 by Emily Carey Alleman. SECOND SPRING by June Masters Bacher. From: QUIET MOMENTS (Harvest House Publishers, 1978). SIESTA by E. Cole Ingle. Previously published in COLUMBUS DISPATCH. SEPTEMBER MORN by Garnett Ann Schultz. From: SOMETHING BEAUTIFUL by Garnett Ann Schultz, Copyright © 1966 by Garnett Ann Schultz. Published by Dorrance & Company. AUTUMN DAYS by Georgia Day Sherwood. From her book: MY WEALTH, Copyright © 1937 by Henry Harrison. Reprinted by permission of Margaret Sherwood. MELANCHOLY SEASON? by Stella Craft Tremble. From her book: PEDDLER'S PACK, Copyright © 1977 by Stella Craft Tremble. THESE by William Arnett Wofford. From his book: CANDLE AT DUSK, Copyright © 1936 by The Banner Press, Emory University, Atlanta, Georgia. Our sincere thanks to the following authors whose addresses we were unable to locate: Catherine E. Berry for: MAGIC from her book: CANDLE IN THE NIGHT, Copyright © 1956; Elsie DeRuiter for OCTOBER RAIN; Jay H. Meyers for INDIAN SUMMER; Marilyn Eynon Scott for AUTUMN MOOD.

Halloween Ghouls

Witches and goblins
And ghosts and such
Don't frighten me,
Don't scare me much!

Tonight's the night
They all come out;
Look out your window—
They're all about.

They cackle and groan
On their brooms. Be wary!
They're either all bone
Or squirmy or hairy.

And, oh—thank heavens!
It's only one night,
And for a little candy
You'll be saved a fright;

For it's the only time
Of the year you'll meet
The Halloween ghosts
Of trick or treat!

Shari Style

A Thanksgiving Heritage . . .

As the geese make their annual migration in late autumn, the season for giving thanks is again upon us. Our richly illustrated Thanksgiving issue features outstanding color photography, poetry and prose which express appreciation for the bountiful blessings we share.

Experience the delightful sights, sounds and smells of the holiday as depicted in "What Is Thanksgiving?" Also share in a college student's heartwarming Thanksgiving homecoming.

Grace Noll Crowell offers praise and gratitude in her prayerful poem "This Is the Land." Featured poems describe the Pilgrims' journey to our shores, reflections on harvesttime and frosty November days. The charming verses of poet Laurie English Dawson capture warm memories of Thanksgivings past.

As always, beautiful illustrations accompany the text. A lovely full-color art reproduction of the Pilgrims' landing is also included.

Express your thankfulness for the many blessings we share by giving a yearly gift subscription to a loved one, friend or relative. If by chance, you are not a subscriber, why not give yourself a year-round gift and start your Ideals collection today.